Also by Dona Z. Meilach

The Best Bagels Are Made at Home
Marinades Make Ordinary Foods Extraordinary
The Best 50 Homemade Liqueurs

Making Your Own Biscotti and Dunking Delights

Making Your Own Biscotti and Dunking Delights

Dona Z. Meilach

Illustrations by
Clair Moritz-Magnesio

Crown Publishers, Inc.
New York

To Brandt Aymar

Published by Crown Publishers, Inc.
201 East 50th Street, New York, New York 10022
Member of the Crown Publishing Group.

Random House, Inc. New York, Toronto, London, Sydney, Auckland

http://www.randomhouse.com/

CROWN is a trademark of Crown Publishers, Inc.

Printed in the United States of America

Design by Nancy Kenmore

Library of Congress Cataloging-in-Publication Data
is available upon request

ISBN 0-517-70495-1

10 9 8 7 6 5 4 3 2 1

First Edition

Acknowledgments

My sincere thanks to Brandt Aymar and the wonderful staff at Crown Publishers with whom I have worked for several years. Each book is given tender loving care that brings it from manuscript to final form.

Special thanks to my daughter, Susan Seligman, of Albuquerque, New Mexico, who helped suggest and test recipes, then made her inimitably insightful comments on my near-finished manuscript. It was a joy working with her in each of our kitchens at various times amid bags of flour, dozens of eggs, and dwindling supplies of nuts, raisins, and chocolate chips.

Thanks to my neighbors, and mostly my fellow Scrabble Club members, who tasted, commented on, and joyfully appreciated the various biscotti I brought in each week.

As always, my unflagging appreciation to my husband, Mel Meilach, for his patience and endurance while the testing and tasting went on and on and despite the fact that there was often little else than biscotti in the freezer.

Contents

A New Romance with Biscotti

Introduction

Thanks to biscotti, dunking has become socially acceptable. These long, dry, semihard cookies with curved tops and flat bottoms are designed for dunking. Their unique texture and taste are perfect for absorbing coffee, tea, punch, wine, and soup. History tells us they evolved about Columbus's time thanks to an Italian baker named Datini who served them with Tuscan wines. The idea spread throughout Italy, and eventually each province became known for a particular flavor.

Biscotti, in Italian, means "twice-baked" (bis-cotti). Baking, then toasting, draws off moisture, resulting in the crisp, dry texture and a long shelf life. Originally, biscotti proved an ideal food for sailors, soldiers, shepherds, and fishermen, all of whom needed sustenance while on long journeys.

Other cultures adapted the concept. Mandelbrot are a version with Jewish origins. The Germans have zweiback; the Spanish have carquinyoles. There are French croquets de carcassonne and Parisienne biscottes, Dutch rusk, and Greek biskota and paximadia.

Today, bakers are turning out biscotti in abundance to accompany our newfound fondness for flavored coffees and teas.

Biscotti are sold in supermarkets, coffeehouses, bakeries, and speciality food shops, often appetizingly displayed in large covered glass jars.

Traditionally, biscotti are almond-flavored because almonds were plentiful in Italy and nearby countries. Now, they may be chock-full of different nuts, dried fruits, chocolate chips, or trail mix. Their tops or sides may be plain, dusted with sugar and cinnamon, frosted with chocolate, white, lemon, or other icings, and decorated with sprinkles, baci *(candy worms), ground nuts, or carefully arranged sliced nuts.*

Biscotti for desserts are sweet; spicy ones are for polite dunking in soups, appetizer dips, and fondues. They are lean, light, and adaptable to our healthy-eating lifestyles. Their grain base and raisins, nuts, and other ingredients give energy and nutrition.

In this book you'll find traditional biscotti recipes and many that are updated to use today's easily available ingredients. Break them up or crumble them for sprinkling on ice cream, puddings, and other desserts. Stuff them so they appear to have an inside and outside layer. Make biscotti piecrusts, too.

Also provided are compatible coffee, wine, soup, and appetizer recipes for imaginative menu additions and a total and delightful dunking experience.

Why Make Biscotti at Home?

With biscotti so plentiful at many gourmet food counters, why make them at home? Because the recipes are easy and fast. And homemade biscotti are economical. A single 3-ounce biscotto in a coffee café might cost $1.00 to $1.50. For the cost of two single pieces, or a 15-ounce package of 8 biscotti in a grocery store ($4.00 to $6.00), you can make a 1½- to 2-pound recipe that yields 20 to 36 pieces.

Biscotti flavors can be varied creatively by mixing and matching fillings, flours, and icings. Make them low-fat by eliminating or reducing butter, oil, or margarine, reducing sugar content, and changing high-calorie nuts to dried fruits, spices, and herbs. Egg whites or egg substitutes for whole eggs will reduce fat and cholesterol. Substitute some of the white flour with granola, muesli, whole wheat, oats, and other flours, too.

Keep a batch of biscotti in a jar or freezer ready for unexpected company or if you need a quick dessert fix. No need to thaw them, either, when you dunk them into hot liquid. Softer varieties are delicious and edible without dunking. They're the perfect answer to "What's there to eat?" when children come in from school or a soccer match. Pack them in your hiker's backpack and in lunch boxes. Bake them for gifts any time of the year.

Procedures and Equipment

Almost all recipes for biscotti involve four basic steps: mix, shape, bake, and cut and rebake.

1. Mix together the butter, sugar, eggs, or similar ingredients; add the dry ingredients; stir in nuts and flavorings.

2. Divide the dough and shape it into logs.

3. Bake the logs.

4. Slice the baked logs diagonally into strips and return them to the oven for a short second baking.

Biscotti can be made in one bowl using only a wire whisk or wooden spoon to mix the ingredients. Modern kitchen appliances such as a food processor, a bread machine, or a food mixer make mixing big biscotti batches easy. A few measuring utensils, cookie sheet, cutting board, and sharp knife are all that are needed.

Storing and Shelf Life

Store biscotti for up to about a week (they often taste better the second day) on the counter or in the refrigerator in an airtight container such as a covered jar, a cookie tin, or a plastic storage baggie. They can go into the freezer at any time—when they're fresh or a few days old—in any freezer wrap or container. Should biscotti become soggy and lose their crispness, retoast them in a toaster unit or in the oven at 250 degrees until they're toasty and crunchy again.

If they are too hard or too dry, place them in a microwave oven at low or defrost setting for half a minute or so.

Ingredients

Anyone who does minimal baking probably has biscotti ingredients on the shelf. Begin with the basic recipe, then follow the other recipes throughout the book. Often, if you're lacking an ingredient, you can substitute something else that you may have.

FLOURS

The recipes offered here will yield excellent results with all-purpose white flour. Unbleached flour and bread flour have a higher gluten content and will yield a slightly more chewy texture. Other grains used include cornmeal, whole wheat, granola, multigrain, and muesli. In high altitudes, a little more flour may be required to achieve the necessary consistency.

BUTTERS AND OILS

Biscotti made with butter are more cakelike and not as hard as those without butter. Use unsalted butter or margarine or mix the two in a recipe. Avoid no-fat products; they have no taste and are too soft to yield a crisp cookie. For vegetable oils use safflower, canola, peanut, or corn oil. For olive oil, select a mild-tasting extra-virgin oil that won't interfere with the delicate flavors of the biscotti.

EGGS

Almost all recipes call for eggs. If you're on a cholesterol-free diet, use egg whites only, adding one extra egg white for every two eggs. Egg substitutes may be used alone or with fresh egg whites.

SWEETENERS

White granulated sugar, brown sugar, turbinado sugar, and honey appear in the recipes. Almond paste can be used in place of sugar, or combined with sugar. (See page 17 for homemade almond paste.) One sugar may be substituted for another.

LEAVENERS AND SALT

Baking powder and baking soda are leaveners, or products that release gases which give the dough its rise. Almost all recipes use double-acting baking powder, some use baking soda, and some use both. Omitting one or the other, or both, will not result in failure, but the taste, texture, and color will change. Salt also alters the biscotti taste but it can be omitted for those on salt-free diets. Baking powder cans are dated. Be sure you use fresh ingredients.

Nuts and Seeds

Almonds, walnuts, hazelnuts, pistachios, chestnuts, raw peanuts, pepitas (pumpkin seeds), and pine nuts give biscotti their variety, flavor, and food value. Sesame, sunflower, and poppy seeds are used frequently. Nuts may be raw, roasted, or blanched. (Avoid salted nuts.) Toasting nuts and seeds lightly before baking brings out their flavor.

Nuts can turn rancid. They should be stored in airtight containers and kept in the refrigerator or freezer. They should always smell fresh and sweet.

Nut flavorings, such as almond, walnut, coconut, and hazelnut, are available as liquid extracts. Hershey's, Nestlé, and other companies provide different-flavored chocolate-covered baking morsels.

How to toast nuts and seeds: Spread nuts or seeds in a single layer on a baking sheet and bake at 300 degrees for 3 to 5 minutes, until slightly darkened. Stir occasionally and turn over. Let cool and slice or chop on a cutting board or use a blender or chopper. Almost all nuts are now sold whole, halved, slivered, chopped, and sliced in small packages. Buying them in bulk will save you money.

Whole hazelnuts are sold in the shell or shelled with the skin on. To remove the skin, toast the shelled nuts as above. When the skins begin to split, remove the nuts from the oven and wrap them in a towel. Rub the nuts with the towel to loosen the skins.

Herbs

For herb-flavored biscotti use fresh or dried basil, rosemary, cloves, fennel, sage, garlic, sun-dried tomato, dried red and green peppers, jalapeño, herbes de Provence, and so forth. Generally, substitute 1 tablespoon fresh herbs for 1 teaspoon dried herbs—a three-to-one ratio.

Fruit Flavorings

In addition to the usual raisins and currants, a huge variety of dried fruits is now available, cut up ready to add to baking mixes. Try dried blueberries, cranberries, dates, figs, peaches, apricots, pineapple, papaya, mango, and other more esoteric varieties available in health food stores and from catalog suppliers. Fold small pieces into the dough. Fresh lemon or orange peel or candied peels may be used also.

Extracts, Liqueurs, Liquors, and Coffee Syrup

Use any of a variety of liquid flavorings. Substitute one for another if you don't have exactly what's called for in the biscotti recipe. Vanilla powder can be substituted for vanilla liquid extract. For almond extract, substitute amaretto liqueur, made from apricot seeds, which has a similar taste. Flavored coffee syrups, available from coffee shops, may be used in caffè latte and espresso recipes, too. When using presweetened flavorings, reduce the amount of sugar called for in the biscotti recipe by about one-eighth.

Favorite liqueur flavors are Kahlúa (coffee), amaretto (apricot), Grand Marnier or Cointreau (orange), and crème de coconut. Optionally, or additionally, use liquors such as rum, whiskey, and brandy: they add interesting flavoring to the recipes. Several traditional recipes use wine, too.

CHOCOLATE

Use a good-quality semisweet chocolate both for chips within the biscotti and for melting, dipping, and icing. (See the icing recipes, pages 20–22.) For darker biscotti and chocolate flavor add a high-quality cocoa powder to the flour. Nestlé Choco Bake is a premelted chocolate that mixes easily with the final dough.

ALMOND PASTE

Almond flavoring, a basic ingredient in traditional biscotti, is available commercially as a paste in tubes and jars and as a liquid extract. You can replace equal portions of sugar with almond paste in any recipe. The following yields 1 pound of almond paste which will keep for several months when stored in a refrigerator.

17

.

1 cup whole almonds	*¼ teaspoon vanilla extract*
1 cup sugar	*½ teaspoon almond extract*
¼ cup water	*Confectioners' sugar*

In a food processor or blender, grind the almonds and sugar until very fine. Add the water and vanilla and almond extracts and blend until a pastelike consistency and forms into a ball. Remove, place on a board lightly dusted with confectioners' sugar, and roll into a 1-inch-diameter log. Wrap in plastic wrap and refrigerate.

Mixing Methods

The ideally mixed biscotti dough becomes a soft ball when it is ready. But humidity, warm weather, and different mixtures can play tricks on even the most experienced baker. Some doughs are sticky and hard to form into a log. Usually, adding a little more flour until a ball forms makes the dough workable, or refrigerate the dough for 10 minutes or so until you can shape it. Coating your hands lightly with vegetable oil or nonstick cooking spray will make working with the dough easier.

HAND MIXING

Place the biscotti ingredients in a large mixing bowl and mix with a wire whisk or a wooden spoon. Hand-mixing requires more time and effort than using a machine. Many people find it therapeutic, like making bread dough by hand.

FOOD PROCESSOR

A food processor makes quick work of mixing a batch of biscotti dough in a single bowl. Be careful about overloading the unit with recipes that are too large for its capacity. Small-capacity units may mix recipes that call for 2 to 3 cups of flour easily. Recipes with 4 to 6 cups of flour require a heavy-duty, large-capacity unit. Most mixers shut off automatically if overloaded. When that happens, divide the recipe in half and mix the halves separately.

BREAD MACHINE

Mix a basic $2\frac{1}{2}$- to 3-cup flour recipe in any size bread machine. Use the machine only to mix, not bake. See chapter 7 for directions and recipes. The bread machine efficiently mixes a homogeneous ball of dough and the one pan and paddle are easy to clean up.

ELECTRIC MIXER

Use the large bowl with an egg beater or paddle attachment for small-capacity recipes (2 to 3 cups of flour). Larger recipes (4 to 6 cups of flour) require a heavy-duty electric mixer rather than a food processor or bread machine, which can also be used for smaller-capacity recipes.

Shaping, Baking, Slicing, and Toasting

SHAPING AND BAKING

Remove the dough from the mixing utensil and place it onto a lightly greased baking sheet. (Nonstick spray works well.) For easy cleanup, line the sheet with parchment paper or aluminum foil.

Divide the dough into two or three parts. Shape each part into a log shape, then flatten into a rectangle about 2 to 4 inches wide, 10 to 12 inches long, and ½ to ¾ inch high, depending on the recipe and the size of biscotti desired. Manipulate with lightly oiled hands or with two rubber spatulas. Allow about 3 inches between the logs; they will spread and rise as they bake.

The log width will determine the biscotti length. Average packaged biscotti are about 3½ to 4 inches long, and gourmet sizes are 6 to 8 inches. Minicookies and mandelbrot are 2½ to 3 inches long.

Place the baking sheet in the center of a preheated oven and bake according to the recipe, usually at 350 degrees for 25 to 30 minutes or until the tops are puffed and lightly browned.

Recipe yields vary depending on the width of the log and the resulting length of the biscotti. Three-cup flour recipes will generally yield 2 to 2½ dozen 5- to 7-inch biscotti and 3 to 4 dozen shorter mandelbrot sizes.

SLICING AND TOASTING

Cool for 10 minutes after removing from the oven, then, using a very sharp knife, slice each log into 45-degree diagonal slices (start at a corner) or straight across for straight slices, about $\frac{5}{8}$ to $\frac{3}{4}$ inches wide. Return the pieces to the baking sheet and lay them cut side down, side by side (it's fine if they touch one another), unless the recipe differs. Toast one side for about 10 minutes, then turn over and bake the second side for about 10 minutes, until browned and crisp to the touch. Some recipes call for standing the pieces upright. Others suggest turning off the oven and letting the cookies dry as the oven cools.

Toppings and Icing

Cool the toasted biscotti about 20 minutes before icing. Add thin icing with a pastry brush. Spread thicker coats with a spatula. Ice the tops of each biscotto or half of a cut side. Dipping one end in melted chocolate is easy to do and looks and tastes great. Drizzle the icing in a pattern over the cut side. Two-color drizzles, chocolate and white, are an attractive touch.

For a fine, consistent drizzle line, melt chocolate in a microwave in a plastic sandwich bag and push it all toward a bottom corner. Cut a small piece off the bottom corner and squeeze the chocolate out as if it were a cake-decorating tube.

Add decorative candy sprinkles to icing. *Baci*, a classic Italian confection, can be chopped up and sprinkled on the icing.

SUGAR TOPPING

Place toasted, cooled biscotti top side up. Use a fine strainer and press $\frac{1}{2}$ to $\frac{3}{4}$ cup confectioners' sugar gently through the strainer while moving the strainer side to side to distribute the sugar evenly. Or dip biscotti tops into a dish of confectioners' sugar.

Option: Mix 2 tablespoons confectioners' sugar with 1 teaspoon ground cinnamon and sprinkle on the logs before or halfway through the baking.

Glaze: Add a shine to the top crust by spreading with beaten egg white on a brush. Or spray lightly with a nonstick vegetable oil.

CHOCOLATE ICING

Method 1: Melt 6 ounces of semisweet chocolate or chocolate chips in a microwave oven on medium for about 1 minute. Stir to blend.

Method 2: Place 6 ounces chopped chocolate in a heat-proof glass baking cup or plastic bag in the top of a double boiler and melt over hot water.

Method 3: Nestlé Choco Bake is premelted and a boon to bakers. For icing combine:

3¼ cups sifted confectioners' sugar
⅓ cup milk
¼ cup (½ stick) softened butter or margarine

2 envelopes Nestlé Choco Bake
2 teaspoons vanilla extract

Beat all the ingredients together in small mixing bowl until smooth and creamy.

Yields 1¾ cups

Lay biscotti on waxed paper when dipping, spreading, or drizzling chocolate. Cool at room temperature until set—about 5 minutes. Let the icing cure and harden for about half an hour before storing. Store frosted biscotti in tins or plastic containers with a layer of waxed paper over the frosted sides to prevent chipping. Refrigerating may turn the chocolate grayish.

White Chocolate or Butterscotch Icing

Same as for dark chocolate, but use white chocolate or butterscotch chips.

Sugar Icing

½ teaspoon flavoring: lemon, vanilla, coconut, and the like

1½ cups confectioners' sugar
6 to 8 teaspoons of milk

Mix together, adding milk until the icing is of drizzling consistency. After icing, let the biscotti set 15 minutes before handling.

Adding Flourishes

- Lay sliced almonds or sliced macadamia nuts on the frosted biscotti in a pattern, or drop on randomly.
- Sprinkle chopped walnuts (medium grind) or other nuts on icing.
- Drizzle strands of white or flavored icing over the sides or tops of biscotti and add colored sprinkles used for cake decorating.
- For special holidays, color white melted chocolate or icing with food coloring: green for Saint Patrick's Day, red and green for Christmas, and so forth.

Basic Almond-Flavored Biscotti

This basic biscotti recipe is delicious plain or with ends dipped into chocolate. Use a combination of sliced and ground almonds for texture.

¼ cup (½ stick) unsalted butter or margarine
1 cup sugar or ¾ cup sugar and ¼ cup almond paste (see page 17)
3 large eggs
1 teaspoon vanilla extract
½ teaspoon almond extract
2 teaspoons orange zest

2½ cups all-purpose flour
1½ teaspoons baking powder
½ teaspoon baking soda
⅛ teaspoon salt
1 teaspoon ground cinnamon
1 cup toasted sliced almonds

Beat together the butter and sugar until fluffy. Beat in the eggs, then blend in the vanilla and almond extracts and orange zest. Add the flour, baking powder, baking soda, salt, and cinnamon and blend until smooth. Fold in the nuts.

Divide the dough in half and shape on a lightly greased baking sheet into two logs about 4 inches wide and ¾ inches high. Place them 2 inches apart. Bake in a 350-degree oven for 25 minutes or until they are lightly puffed and browned. Cool for 10 minutes in the pan, then transfer to a cutting board. Cut each log diagonally into ¾-inch slices. Place the slices cut side down on a baking sheet. Toast each side in a 275-degree oven for 10 minutes, until golden brown. Cool.

Yields about 2½ dozen biscotti

Low-Fat
Almond–Poppy Seed Biscotti

You'll be delighted at how easy these biscotti are to make. They're a variation on the classic biscotti di Prato that originated in the medieval town of Prato, near Florence. In Prato they are served for dipping into Vin Santo, an amber-colored dessert wine. No butter is used in this low-fat recipe.

3 large eggs or 4 egg whites	½ teaspoon baking soda
¾ cup sugar	¼ teaspoon salt
1 teaspoon orange zest	1 cup toasted almonds,
1½ teaspoons vanilla extract	coarsely chopped
2½ cups all-purpose flour	2 tablespoons poppy seed
1 teaspoon baking powder	

Beat together the eggs and sugar until light and foamy. Beat in the orange zest and vanilla. Add the flour, baking powder, baking soda, and salt and blend until smooth. Stir in the almonds and poppy seed.

Divide the dough in half and shape on a lightly greased baking sheet into two logs about 3½ inches wide and ¾ inches high. Place them 4 inches apart and smooth the tops and sides with a rubber spatula or with oiled fingers. Bake at 325 degrees for 30 minutes or until golden brown. Cool for 10 minutes. Transfer to a cutting board. Cut each log diagonally into ½- or ¾-inch slices. Place the slices cut side down on a baking sheet. Toast each side at 275 degrees for 10 minutes or until lightly toasted. Cool.

Yields about 2½ dozen biscotti

Almond-Lemon Biscotti

The lemon flavoring offsets the sweetness in this classic Italian recipe.

5 egg whites
1 cup vegetable oil
1 cup sugar
1 tablespoon almond paste
   (optional; see page 17)
3/4 teaspoon lemon extract
3/4 teaspoon almond extract
1 tablespoon grated or
   finely diced lemon peel
3 cups all-purpose flour

2 teaspoons baking powder
1/8 teaspoon salt
1 cup toasted sliced
   almonds

TOPPING
1 teaspoon sugar
1/2 teaspoon ground
   cinnamon
1/2 teaspoon nutmeg

Beat the egg whites until fluffy. Add the oil, sugar, and almond paste, if using, and blend thoroughly. Mix in the lemon and almond extracts and lemon peel. Add the flour, baking powder, and salt and blend until smooth. Fold in the almonds.

Divide the dough into thirds, drop by large spoonfuls onto a lightly greased baking sheet, and shape into logs about 4 inches wide and 3/4 inches high. Place them 2 inches apart. Bake in a 350-degree oven for 25 minutes, until lightly browned. For the topping, mix the sugar, cinnamon, and nutmeg and sprinkle on the logs after 15 minutes of baking. Cool for 10 minutes. Transfer to a cutting board and cut diagonally into 1/2- to 3/4-inch slices. Place the slices cut side down on a baking sheet, turn off the heat, and return to the oven for 10 minutes on each side, or until golden brown. Cool.

Yields 2 1/2 to 3 dozen biscotti

Turkish Delight Almond-Apricot Biscotti

Turkey, known for its assorted "Turkish delight" cookies and confections filled with fruits and nuts, inspired this biscotti variation. Flecks of apricots dot the dough. Spread with lemon-flavored sugar icing (see "Sugar Icings," page 22).

1/4 cup (1/2 stick) unsalted butter or margarine
3/4 cup sugar
1/4 cup almond paste (see page 17)
3 large eggs
1 teaspoon vanilla extract
3 cups all-purpose flour
1 teaspoon baking powder
1/8 teaspoon salt
3/4 cup raw shelled pistachios
3/4 cup toasted sliced almonds
3/4 cup diced dried apricots

Beat together the butter, sugar, and almond paste until light and fluffy. Beat in the eggs and vanilla. Add the flour, baking powder, and salt and blend until smooth. Fold in the nuts and apricots.

Divide the dough in half on a lightly greased baking sheet and shape each half into a log about 3 inches wide and 5/8 to 3/4 inches high. Place the logs 3 inches apart. Bake in a 350-degree oven for 25 minutes or until they are lightly puffed and browned. Cool for 10 minutes. Transfer to a cutting board and cut each log diagonally into 5/8-inch slices. Place the slices cut side down on a baking sheet. Toast each side in a 275-degree oven for 10 minutes or until golden brown. Cool.

Yields 2 1/2 to 3 dozen biscotti

Triple-Threat Nut Biscotti Dipped in Chocolate

The extra taste and crunch of almonds plus the pecans and raw white peanuts yield a triple-flavor winner.

1/4 cup (1/2 stick) unsalted
    butter or margarine
3/4 cup sugar
3 large eggs
1 teaspoon vanilla extract
1/2 teaspoon almond extract
1 tablespoon each grated
    orange and lemon peel
3 cups unbleached or
    all-purpose flour

1 teaspoon baking soda
1/8 teaspoon salt
1/2 cup toasted sliced
    almonds
1/3 cup toasted pecans,
    coarsely chopped
1/3 cup toasted raw peanuts,
    chopped
1 1/2 cups white or brown
    chocolate chips, melted

Cream together the butter and sugar until fluffy. Beat in the eggs, then the vanilla and almond extracts and citrus peels. Add the flour, baking soda, and salt and blend until smooth. Fold in the nuts.

Divide the dough in half or thirds on a lightly greased baking sheet and shape each piece into a log about 2 1/2 inches wide and 3/4 inches high. Place the logs 3 inches apart. Bake in a 350-degree oven for 25 minutes or until they are lightly puffed and browned. Cool for 10 minutes. Transfer to a cutting board and cut each log diagonally into 3/4-inch slices. Place the slices cut side down on a baking sheet. Toast each side in a 275-degree oven for 10 minutes or until golden brown. Cool. Dip the ends in melted chocolate and cool on a rack.

Yields about 2 1/2 to 3 dozen biscotti

Almond-Ginger Biscotti

Ginger in three different forms—fresh ginger root, ginger powder, and crystallized ginger—results in biscotti with an extra-spicy bite.

1/4 cup (1/2 stick) unsalted
  butter or margarine
1 cup sugar
3 large eggs
1/2 teaspoon almond extract
2 tablespoons peeled and
  grated fresh ginger root
3 cups unbleached or
  all-purpose flour
1 teaspoon baking powder

1/2 teaspoon baking soda
1/8 teaspoon salt
1/2 teaspoon ground
  cinnamon
1 teaspoon ground ginger
  powder
1 1/4 cups toasted sliced
  almonds
1 cup coarsely chopped
  crystallized ginger

Cream together the butter and sugar until fluffy. Beat in the eggs, then blend in the almond extract and ginger root. Add the flour, baking powder, baking soda, salt, cinnamon, and ground ginger and blend well. Stir in the almonds and the crystallized ginger.

Divide the dough in half or thirds and shape on a lightly greased baking sheet into logs about 2 inches wide and 3/4 inches high. Place the logs 2 inches apart. Bake in a 350-degree oven 25 to 30 minutes or until they are lightly puffed on top. Cool for 10 minutes. Transfer to a cutting board and cut into 3/4-inch slices. Place the slices cut side down on a baking sheet and return them to the oven, turning off the heat. Toast for 15 minutes on each side or until golden brown. Cool.

Yields about 3 dozen biscotti

Cakelike Almond Biscotti

These cakelike biscotti are wonderful for dipping into dessert fondues. They are easier to bite into than the harder cookies and good for snacking without dipping, too.

$\frac{1}{4}$ cup ($\frac{1}{2}$ stick) unsalted
 butter or margarine
$\frac{1}{2}$ cup almond paste (see
 page 17)
$\frac{1}{2}$ cup sugar
2 large eggs
$\frac{1}{2}$ teaspoon lemon extract
$\frac{1}{2}$ teaspoon vanilla extract

1 tablespoon finely diced
 lemon zest (peel)
3 cups unbleached or
 all-purpose flour
$\frac{1}{2}$ teaspoon baking powder
$\frac{1}{8}$ teaspoon salt
1 cup toasted sliced
 almonds

Beat together the butter, almond paste, and sugar until creamy. Mix in the eggs, then the lemon and vanilla extracts and lemon peel. Add the flour, baking powder, and salt and blend until smooth. Fold in the almonds.

Divide the dough in half and shape on a lightly greased baking sheet into two logs about 4 inches wide and $\frac{3}{4}$ inches high. Place them 2 inches apart. Bake in a 350-degree oven for 25 minutes or until they are lightly puffed and browned. Cool for 10 minutes. Transfer to a cutting board and cut each log diagonally into $\frac{3}{4}$-inch slices. Place the slices cut side down on a baking sheet. Toast each side in a 275-degree oven for 10 minutes or until golden brown. Cool.

Yields about 2 dozen biscotti

CHAPTER

3

Chocolate
Lovers'
Biscotti

Gourmet coffee house owners report that next to plain white almond-flavored biscotti, anything with chocolate comes in a close second.

Chocolate Mardi Gras Biscotti

These aren't traditional, but they are up-to-date and festive, using M&M multicolored baking candies from your supermarket, a hint of Kahlúa, and a scent of orange.

³⁄₄ cup sugar	¹⁄₄ cup unsweetened Dutch
3 large eggs	cocoa powder
2 tablespoons Kahlúa	1¹⁄₂ teaspoons baking powder
1 teaspoon orange zest	¹⁄₂ teaspoon baking soda
2¹⁄₂ cups unbleached or	¹⁄₈ teaspoon salt
all-purpose flour	1¹⁄₄ cups multicolored M&M
	baking candies

Beat together the sugar and eggs until light and fluffy. Mix in the Kahlúa and orange zest. Add the flour, cocoa, baking powder, baking soda, and salt and blend until smooth. Fold in the M&M candies.

Divide the dough in half and shape on a lightly greased baking sheet into two logs about 4 inches wide and ³⁄₄ inches high. Place them 4 inches apart. Bake in a 350-degree oven for about 25 minutes. Cool for 10 minutes. Transfer to a cutting board. Cut each log diagonally into ³⁄₄-inch slices. Turn off the oven and stand the biscotti up on a baking sheet, return to the oven, and allow to dry out for about 30 minutes. Cool.

Yields 2 dozen biscotti

Chocolate Coconut-Almond Biscotti

For an international appeal, add Hawaiian flavors to Italian cookies.

3 large eggs
¾ cup sugar, plus additional for sprinkling
2 tablespoons unsalted butter or margarine
1 teaspoon vanilla extract
1 teaspoon coconut extract
2⅓ cups unbleached or all-purpose flour
3 tablespoons unsweetened Dutch cocoa powder

1 teaspoon baking powder
½ teaspoon baking soda
⅛ teaspoon salt
1 cup Hershey's chocolate-covered coconut and almond baking bits
¾ cup toasted sliced almonds

1 egg, beaten with 2 tablespoons of water

Cream together the eggs and ¾ cup of sugar; add the butter and vanilla and coconut extracts and beat well. Add the flour, cocoa, baking powder, baking soda, and salt and blend well. Fold in the baking bits and almonds.

Divide the dough in half and shape on a lightly greased baking sheet into two logs about 3 inches wide and ¾ inches high. Place them 3 inches apart. Brush with the egg wash and lightly sprinkle with sugar. Bake at 350 degrees for 25 minutes or until puffed and lightly browned on top. Cool for 10 minutes. Transfer to a cutting board. Cut each log diagonally into ½-inch slices. Place the slices cut side down on a baking sheet. Toast each side in a 300-degree oven for 10 minutes. Cool.

Yields 2½ dozen biscotti

Hazelnut Chocolate-Iced Biscotti

Hazelnuts have long been a favorite biscotti ingredient instead of, or combined with, almonds. Hazelnut biscotti, called *biscotti di nocciole*, have many variations. Packaged chopped hazelnuts simplify the recipe. Top with White Chocolate Icing (see page 22).

¾ cup sugar	*1½ teaspoons baking powder*
3 large eggs	*½ teaspoon baking soda*
1 teaspoon vanilla extract	*⅛ teaspoon salt*
2 tablespoons orange liqueur	*1 cup skinned and coarsely chopped hazelnuts, toasted*
1 teaspoon orange zest	
2½ cups all-purpose flour	

Beat together the sugar and eggs until fluffy. Mix in the vanilla, orange liqueur, and orange zest. Add the flour, baking powder, baking soda, and salt and blend well. Fold in the nuts.

Divide the dough in half and shape on a lightly greased baking sheet into two logs about 3 inches wide and ¾ inches high. Place them 3 inches apart. Bake at 350 degrees for 20 to 25 minutes, until puffed and crusty on top. Cool for 10 minutes. Transfer to a cutting board. Cut each log diagonally into ½- or ¾-inch slices. Place the slices cut side down on a baking sheet and toast each side at 275 degrees for 10 minutes. Cool.

Yields 3 dozen biscotti

Double Chocolate Walnut-Raisin Biscotti

Chocolate dough combined with chocolate chips, nuts, and raisins creates an ultimate taste treat for chocoholics. Dip the biscotti ends into dark or white chocolate icing (see pages 21–22 for recipes).

3 large eggs	*1 teaspoon baking soda*
³⁄₄ cup sugar	*¹⁄₈ teaspoon salt*
1 teaspoon vanilla extract	*³⁄₄ cup coarsely chopped*
¹⁄₂ teaspoon almond extract	*walnuts, toasted*
3 cups unbleached or	*¹⁄₂ cup mini semisweet*
all-purpose flour	*chocolate chips*
¹⁄₃ cup unsweetened Dutch	*¹⁄₂ cup raisins*
cocoa powder	

Beat together the eggs and sugar until light and fluffy. Add the vanilla and almond extracts. Add the flour, cocoa, baking soda, and salt and blend until smooth. Fold in the nuts, chocolate chips, and raisins.

Divide the dough in half and shape on a lightly greased baking sheet into two logs about 4 inches wide and ³⁄₄ inches high. Place them 2 inches apart. Bake at 300 degrees for 50 minutes or until the tops appear puffed and lightly cracked. Cool for 10 minutes. Transfer to a cutting board. Cut each log diagonally into ¹⁄₂- or ³⁄₄-inch slices. Place the slices cut side down on a baking sheet and toast each side in a 275-degree oven for 10 minutes or until golden brown. Cool.

Yields about 3 dozen biscotti

Chocolate Mocha-Peanut Biscotti

Nothing traditional about this, but a simple sinful combination of flavors. They're wonderful dipped in milk or coffee. Try them, too, spread with, or dipped into, low-calorie whipped topping.

¼ cup (½ stick) unsalted butter or margarine
¼ cup cream cheese
1 cup sugar
2 large eggs
¼ cup espresso beans finely ground as for coffee
¼ cup brewed espresso (or double-strength coffee or 2 tablespoons Kahlúa)

2½ cups unbleached or all-purpose flour
1 teaspoon baking powder
½ teaspoon baking soda
⅛ teaspoon salt
⅔ cup raw peanuts (unsalted, unroasted)
¾ cup mini semisweet chocolate or peanut butter chips

Beat together the butter, cream cheese, and sugar until creamy. Beat in the eggs, then the ground coffee and brewed coffee or Kahlúa. Add the flour, baking powder, baking soda, and salt and mix until well blended. Fold in the peanuts and chips.

Divide the dough in half and shape on a lightly greased baking sheet into two logs about 4 inches wide and ¾ inches high. Place them 3 inches apart. Bake in a 350-degree oven for 25 minutes or until the top appears lightly cracked. Cool for 10 minutes. Transfer to a cutting board. Cut each log diagonally into ¾-inch slices. Place the slices cut side down on a baking sheet and toast each side in a 275-degree oven for 10 minutes or until crisp. Cool completely before storing.

Yields 2½ dozen biscotti

Chocolate Walnut-Anise Biscotti

Anise provides a delightfully luscious licorice taste and aroma. White chocolate chips contrast with the chocolate color.

3 teaspoons aniseed
1/4 cup vermouth
1/4 cup (1/2 stick) unsalted
    butter or margarine
1 cup sugar
3 large eggs
1 teaspoon anise extract
2 1/2 cups all-purpose flour
1 teaspoon baking powder

1/2 teaspoon baking soda
1/8 teaspoon salt
1/4 cup unsweetened Dutch
    cocoa powder
1 cup coarsely chopped
    walnuts
1 cup mini white chocolate
    chips or chopped white
    chocolate

Soak the aniseed in the vermouth overnight. Cream together the butter and sugar until fluffy. Beat in the eggs and anise extract. Add the flour, baking powder, baking soda, salt, and cocoa to the creamed mixture. Mix in the aniseed. Fold in the walnuts and white chocolate pieces.

Divide the dough in half and shape on a lightly greased baking sheet into two logs about 3 inches wide and 1/2 to 3/4 inches high. Place them 3 inches apart. Bake in a 350-degree oven for 25 minutes or until the tops are puffy. Cool for 10 minutes. Transfer the logs to a cutting board and cut into 1/2- or 3/4-inch slices. Stand the cookies up and toast 10 minutes in a 275-degree oven. Cool.

Yields about 3 dozen biscotti

Chocolate Chip–Pistachio Biscotti

Pistachio nuts, chocolate chips, and raisins make a delectable dunking combination.

³/₄ cup (5¹/₂ tablespoons) unsalted butter or margarine
1 cup sugar or ¹/₂ cup granulated sugar and ¹/₂ cup brown
2 large eggs
1 teaspoon almond extract
1¹/₂ cups unbleached or all-purpose flour
1 cup whole wheat flour

1 teaspoon ground cinnamon
1 teaspoon baking powder
¹/₄ teaspoon baking soda
¹/₈ teaspoon salt
³/₄ cup raw pistachio nuts, coarsely chopped
1 cup mini semisweet chocolate chips
³/₄ cup golden raisins

Cream together the butter and sugar until fluffy. Mix in the eggs and almond extract and blend. Add the flours, cinnamon, baking powder, baking soda, and salt and mix well. Fold in the nuts, chocolate chips, and raisins.

Divide the dough in half and shape on a lightly greased baking sheet into two logs about 3 inches wide and ⁵/₈ inches high. Place them 3 inches apart. Bake in a 350-degree oven for 25 minutes or until they are lightly puffed and crusty on top. Cool for 10 minutes. Transfer to a cutting board and cut into ⁵/₈-inch slices. Lay the pieces flat on a baking sheet and return to the oven (turn off the heat) for 10 minutes on each side, letting them brown as the oven cools. Cool.

Yields 2¹/₂ to 3 dozen biscotti

White Chocolate–Orange-Macadamia Nut Biscotti

A blending of wonderful flavors makes this recipe a favorite. It's especially good with White Chocolate Icing (see page 22).

1/4 cup (1/2 stick) unsalted butter or margarine

3/4 cup sugar

3 large eggs

1 teaspoon vanilla extract

2 tablespoons orange zest

2 tablespoons orange liqueur

2 1/4 cups unbleached or all-purpose flour

1 teaspoon baking powder

1/8 teaspoon salt

2/3 cup sliced macadamia nuts

1 cup white chocolate chips

Cream together the butter and sugar until fluffy. Beat in the eggs, vanilla extract, and orange zest and liqueur. Add the flour, baking powder, and salt to the creamed mixture and blend until smooth. Fold in the nuts and chips.

Divide the dough in half and shape on a lightly greased baking sheet into two logs about 4 inches wide and 3/4 inches high. Place them 3 inches apart. Bake in a 350-degree oven for 25 to 30 minutes or until they are lightly browned. Cool in the pan for 10 minutes. Transfer to a cutting board and cut into 1/2- to 3/4-inch slices. Stand the slices up on a baking sheet and return to the oven (turn off the heat) for 20 to 30 minutes. Cool.

Yields 2 to 2 1/2 dozen biscotti

Layered Chocolate-Coconut Biscotti

Double-layered biscotti of white and chocolate dough are easy to make and attractive. Fill the white layer with dark chocolate chips and both layers with coconut and golden raisins.

3 large eggs
1 cup sugar
2 tablespoons vegetable oil
1 teaspoon lemon juice
1 teaspoon coconut extract
2¾ cups unbleached or
    all-purpose flour
1½ teaspoons baking powder
½ teaspoon baking soda

⅛ teaspoon salt
½ cup flaked coconut
1 cup golden raisins
1 envelope (1 ounce) Nestlé
    Choco Bake (or 1 ounce
    melted chocolate or 2
    tablespoons unsweetened
    cocoa powder)
½ cup white chocolate chips

Beat together the eggs and sugar until fluffy. Mix in the oil, lemon juice, and coconut extract and blend well. Add the flour, baking powder, baking soda, and salt and blend until smooth. Fold in the coconut and raisins. Remove half of the dough from the bowl onto an aluminum foil–lined baking sheet (if sticky, refrigerate for about 10 minutes). Shape into a log and flatten to about 3½ to 4 inches wide, ⅜ inches high, and about 15 inches long.

Add the chocolate flavoring to the remaining dough in the mixing bowl and mix until the dough turns chocolate-colored. Fold in the white chocolate chips. Remove the dough from the bowl and make a log next to and the same size as the white log. Using the foil to lift, flip the white log on top of the chocolate log. Press them together lightly and smooth the top and edges. Bake in the oven at 350 degrees for 25 to 30 minutes. Cool for 10 minutes. Transfer to a cutting board and slice the combined log diagonally into ½- to ¾-inch slices. Stand the slices up on a baking sheet and return to oven to toast for about 10 minutes on each side. Cool.

Yields 2 dozen biscotti

Optional: Spread melted chocolate on the tops of the slices.

Marbleized Mocha-Almond Biscotti

Certainly two-tone biscotti will intrigue the eye. They're a snap to make and it's fun to watch the designs emerge.

¼ cup (½ stick) unsalted butter or margarine
1 cup sugar
3 large eggs
¼ cup brewed espresso or double-strength coffee
3 cups unbleached or all-purpose flour

1½ teaspoons baking powder
⅛ teaspoon salt
4 tablespoons espresso beans, coarsely ground
1¼ cups sliced toasted almonds
1 envelope Nestlé Choco Bake

Beat together the butter and sugar until fluffy. Mix in the eggs, then add the coffee and blend well. Add the flour, baking powder, and salt and mix until smooth. Blend in the espresso beans and almonds. Stir in Choco Bake, but only until the dough has a marbleized appearance.

Divide the dough in half and shape on a lightly greased baking sheet into two logs about 4 inches wide and ¾ inches high. Place them 3 inches apart. Bake in a 350-degree oven for 25 to 30 minutes or until they are lightly puffed on top. Cool for 10 minutes. Transfer the logs to a cutting board and cut diagonally into ¾-inch slices. Stand the slices up on a baking sheet and return to the oven (turn off the heat) for 30 to 40 minutes. Cool.

Yields 2½ dozen biscotti

CHAPTER

4

*Fruits
and Other
"Funtastic"
Flavors*

Although almonds are the traditional addition to biscotti, other ingredients can contribute variety and nourishment. Raisins are an obvious mate for nuts, but any other available dried fruits alone or in combination are a boon to biscotti bakers.

Trail Mix Biscotti

Try your favorite trail mix embedded in biscotti. There are varieties with all fruits, fruits and nuts, nuts, raisins, and M&Ms.

$1/4$ cup ($1/2$ stick) unsalted butter or margarine
$3/4$ cup sugar
3 large eggs
1 teaspoon lemon zest
$1^{1}/_{2}$ teaspoons vanilla extract

3 cups all-purpose flour
1 teaspoon baking powder
$1/2$ teaspoon baking soda
$1/8$ teaspoon salt
$1^{1}/_{2}$ cups trail mix

Cream together the butter and sugar until fluffy. Blend in the eggs, then the lemon zest and vanilla. Add the flour, baking powder, baking soda, and salt and blend until smooth. Fold in the trail mix.

Divide the dough in half and shape on a lightly greased baking sheet into two logs about 4 inches wide and $5/8$ to $3/4$ inches high. Place them 3 inches apart. Bake in a 350-degree oven for 25 to 30 minutes or until they are golden brown. Cool for 10 minutes. Transfer to a cutting board and cut each log diagonally into $3/4$-inch slices. Place the slices cut side down on a baking sheet and toast each side in a 275-degree oven for 10 minutes. Cool.

Yields about 2 to $2^{1}/_{2}$ dozen biscotti

Hiker's Health Biscotti

Fill biscotti with a mixed dry fruit medley and pack it as a snack in your hiker's bag. It's ideal for breakfast, too, and as an energy picker-upper any time of the day.

¼ cup (½ stick) unsalted butter or margarine
1 cup brown sugar
3 large eggs
1 teaspoon vanilla extract
1 cup whole wheat flour
2 cups unbleached or all-purpose flour
1 teaspoon baking powder
⅛ teaspoon salt

1 tablespoon ground cinnamon
1 cup toasted walnuts or pecans, coarsely chopped
1½ cups dried fruit medley, diced small (ready packaged, or combine any dried fruits available, such as dates, figs, cranberries, or blueberries)

Cream together the butter and sugar until fluffy. Beat in the eggs and vanilla. Add the flours, baking powder, salt, and cinnamon and blend until smooth. Fold in the nuts and dried fruits.

Divide the dough in half and shape on a lightly greased baking sheet into two logs about 4 inches wide and ⅝ to ¾ inches high. Place them 3 inches apart. Bake in a 350-degree oven for 25 to 30 minutes or until they are crusty on top. Cool for 10 minutes. Transfer to a cutting board and cut each log diagonally into ½- to ¾-inch slices. Place the slices cut side down on a baking sheet and toast each side in a 275-degree oven for 10 minutes. Cool.

Yields about 2 dozen biscotti

Blueberry-Muesli-Nut Biscotti

A breakfast cereal can become a biscotti basis. Muesli may be packaged with different fruits and nuts such as strawberries or blueberries, and pecans. These may be used with or without additional dried fruits.

1/4 cup (1/2 stick) unsalted butter or margarine	1/2 teaspoon baking soda
1 cup brown sugar	1/8 teaspoon salt
3 large eggs	1 tablespoon ground cinnamon
1 teaspoon almond extract	1 cup dried blueberries
2 cups muesli	1 cup raw pistachio nuts
2 1/2 cups unbleached or all-purpose flour	1/2 cup toasted almonds, coarsely chopped
1 teaspoon baking powder	

Cream together the butter and sugar until fluffy. Beat in the eggs and almond extract. Add the muesli, flour, baking powder, baking soda, salt, and cinnamon and blend until smooth. Fold in the dried fruit and nuts.

Divide the dough in half and shape on a lightly greased baking sheet into two logs about 4 inches wide and 5/8 to 3/4 inches high. Place them 3 inches apart. Bake in the oven at 350 degrees for 25 to 30 minutes or until golden brown. Cool for 10 minutes. Transfer to a cutting board and cut each log diagonally into 3/4-inch slices. Place the slices cut side down on a baking sheet and toast each side in a 275-degree oven for 10 minutes. Cool.

Yields about 3 dozen biscotti

Cranberry-Pistachio Biscotti

Try these at Thanksgiving time for a new twist to your holiday meal or anytime cranberries are available. Use any other dried fruits such as cherries, dates, figs, or raisins, too.

*½ cup (1 stick) unsalted
   butter or margarine
1 cup brown sugar
3 large eggs
1 teaspoon vanilla extract
2½ cups unbleached or
   all-purpose flour
1 teaspoon baking powder*

*⅛ teaspoon salt
1 tablespoon ground
   cinnamon
1 cup raw pistachio nuts
1 cup dried cranberries or
   2 cups coarsely chopped
   fresh cranberries*

Cream together the butter and sugar until fluffy. Beat in the eggs and vanilla. Add the flour, baking powder, salt, and cinnamon to the creamed mixture and blend until smooth. Fold in the nuts and cranberries.

Divide the dough in half and shape on a lightly greased baking sheet into two logs about 4 inches wide and ⅝ to ¾ inches high. Place them 3 inches apart. Bake in a 350-degree oven for 25 to 30 minutes or until they are golden brown. Cool for 10 minutes. Transfer to a cutting board and cut each log diagonally into ¾-inch slices. Place the slices cut side down on a baking sheet and toast each side in a 275-degree oven for 10 minutes. Cool.

Yields about 2½ dozen biscotti

Date and Nut Biscotti

Biscotti filled with dried dates and nuts are nutritious and perfect for a midafternoon energy snack with a cup of coffee, tea, or hot chocolate.

½ cup (1 stick) unsalted
  butter or margarine
1 cup sugar
3 large eggs
1 teaspoon lemon zest
1 teaspoon vanilla extract
3¼ cups unbleached or
  all-purpose flour
1 teaspoon baking powder

⅛ teaspoon salt
½ cup toasted walnuts,
  coarsely chopped
½ cup toasted almonds,
  coarsely chopped
¾ cup chopped dates lightly
  coated with 2 tablespoons
  flour

Cream together the butter and sugar until fluffy. Blend in the eggs, lemon zest, and vanilla. Add the flour, baking powder, and salt and blend until smooth. Fold in the nuts and powdered dates.

Divide the dough in half and shape on a lightly greased baking sheet into two logs about 4 inches wide and ⅝ to ¾ inches high. Place them 3 inches apart. Bake in the oven at 350 degrees for 25 to 30 minutes or until golden brown. Cool for 10 minutes. Transfer to a cutting board and cut each log diagonally into ¾-inch slices. Place the slices cut side down on a baking sheet and toast each side in a 275-degree oven for 10 minutes or until lightly crusty on top. Cool.

Yields about 3 dozen biscotti

Hearty, Crunchy Granola Biscotti

Granola, available in a box or by the pound from a health food store, is made from oatmeal combined with different fruits such as blueberries, raspberries, or strawberries. It's a crunchy, munchy taste treat.

½ cup (1 stick) unsalted
butter or margarine
1 cup brown sugar
3 large eggs
1 teaspoon almond extract
3 cups unbleached or
all-purpose flour

1 teaspoon baking powder
⅛ teaspoon salt
1 teaspoon ground
cinnamon
1 cup granola
1 cup toasted sliced
almonds

Cream together the butter and sugar until fluffy. Beat in the eggs and almond extract. Add the flour, baking powder, salt, and cinnamon and blend until smooth. Fold in the granola and almonds.

Divide the dough in half and shape on a lightly greased baking sheet into two logs about 4 inches wide and ⅝ to ¾ inches high. Place them 3 inches apart. Bake at 350 degrees for 25 to 30 minutes or until golden brown. Cool for 10 minutes. Transfer to a cutting board and cut each log diagonally into ¾-inch slices. Place the slices cut side down on a baking sheet and toast each side in a 275-degree oven for 10 minutes. Cool.

Yields about 3 dozen biscotti

Apple-Cinnamon-Raisin Biscotti

Healthy, low-fat, tasty biscotti bursting with dried fruits and nuts are perfect for restoring energy after a workout or anytime you need a quick pick-me-up.

¾ cup sugar
3 large eggs
2 tablespoons brandy
1 teaspoon vanilla extract
3 cups all-purpose flour
1½ teaspoons baking powder
½ teaspoon baking soda

⅛ teaspoon salt
1 teaspoon ground cinnamon
¾ cup golden raisins
½ cup chopped dried apples
½ cup raw pistachio nuts

Cream together the sugar and eggs until light and fluffy. Blend in the brandy and vanilla. Add the flour, baking powder, baking soda, salt, and cinnamon and blend until smooth. Fold in the raisins, apples, and pistachios.

Divide the dough in half and shape on a lightly greased baking sheet into two logs about 4 inches wide and ⅝ to ¾ inches high. Place them 3 inches apart. Bake in a 350-degree oven for 20 to 25 minutes or until they are golden brown. Cool for 10 minutes. Transfer to a cutting board and cut each log diagonally into ¾-inch slices. Place the slices cut side down on a baking sheet and toast each side in a 275-degree oven for 10 minutes. Cool.

Yields about 2 dozen biscotti

Valentine Biscotti

Here's the perfect gift for your Valentine. Embed colored cake sprinkles and cinnamon hearts in the biscotti dough.

*¼ cup (½ stick) unsalted
  butter or margarine*
¾ cup sugar
3 large eggs
*1 teaspoon vanilla
  extract*
*3¼ cups unbleached or
  all-purpose flour*
1 teaspoon baking powder
⅛ teaspoon salt

*2 tablespoons red candy
  sprinkles*
1 cup red heart candies

ICING
*1½ cups melted white
  chocolate chips*
2–3 drops red food coloring
*1 teaspoon multicolored
  candy sprinkles*

Cream together the butter and sugar until fluffy. Blend in the eggs and vanilla. Add the flour, baking powder, and salt, and blend until smooth. Fold in the sprinkles and heart candies.

Divide the dough in half and shape on a lightly greased baking sheet into two logs about 4 inches wide and ⅝ to ¾ inches high. Place them 3 inches apart. Bake in a 350-degree oven for 25 to 30 minutes or until they are golden brown. Cool for 10 minutes. Transfer to a cutting board and cut each log diagonally into ¾-inch slices. Stand the slices up on a baking sheet and toast in the hot oven (turn off the heat) about 30 minutes or until lightly browned. Cool.

For the icing, melt the chocolate and food coloring and spread on the biscotti tops. Distribute the multicolored sprinkles onto the icing.

Yields about 2½ dozen biscotti

Colorful Panettone Biscotti

An Italian Christmas bread inspired these biscotti, chock-full of colored chunks of candied pineapple, citron, cherries, and lemon and orange peel. Serve them with eggnog or hot cider.

3/4 cup sugar
1/2 cup almond paste (see page 17)
3 large eggs
2 tablespoons unsalted butter or margarine
1 teaspoon vanilla extract
3 tablespoons rum
3 cups unbleached or all-purpose flour

1 teaspoon baking powder
1/2 teaspoon baking soda
1/8 teaspoon salt
1 1/2 cups glacé cake mix (or chopped green and red cherries)
1/2 cup toasted sliced almonds

Cream together the sugar, almond paste, and eggs until light and fluffy. Add the butter and blend well. Blend in the vanilla and rum flavoring. Add the flour, baking powder, baking soda, and salt and blend until smooth. Fold in the glacé mix and almonds.

Divide the dough in half and shape on a lightly greased baking sheet into two logs about 4 inches wide and 5/8 to 3/4 inches high. Place them 3 inches apart. Bake in the oven at 350 degrees for 25 to 30 minutes or until golden brown. Cool for 10 minutes. Transfer to a cutting board and cut each log diagonally into 3/4-inch slices. Place the slices cut side down on a baking sheet and toast each side in a 275-degree oven for 10 minutes. Cool.

Yields about 2 1/2 dozen biscotti

CHAPTER

5

*Piquant
Herb, Spice,
and Nut
Biscotti*

Breadsticks and crackers, move over. We've translated the sweet dessert biscotti into a crunchy, munchy, savory accompaniment for soups, appetizers, and salads. Adding herbs, spices, and vegetables, cheeses and chile, yields a new taste treat that will add variety to your menus.

Green Chili Cheese and Corn Biscotti

The flavors of New Mexico blend beautifully for spicy biscotti that will perk up a Mexican buffet table.

2½ cups all-purpose flour
1½ teaspoons baking powder
¼ teaspoon salt
2 large eggs
3 tablespoons unsalted butter
½ cup vegetable or olive oil

½ cup shredded colby or jack cheese
½ cup diced fresh green chile (or drained, blotted canned)
½ cup kernel corn

In a large bowl or a food processor, mix together the flour, baking powder, and salt. Add the eggs, butter, oil, and cheese and blend. Fold in the chile and corn.

Remove the dough from the bowl and place it on a lightly greased baking sheet. Divide the dough in half and shape into two logs about 3 inches wide and 12 inches long. Place them about 2 inches apart. Bake in a 350-degree oven for 25 minutes or until they are lightly browned. Cool for 10 minutes. Transfer to a cutting board and slice into narrow sticks and toast in a 275-degree oven for 10 minutes on each side. Remove when the oven has cooled.

Yields 2½ to 3 dozen biscotti

Rosemary-Walnut Biscotti

Rosemary and walnuts team up for flavorful, crunchy biscotti that are terrific with wines, appetizer dips, soups, and salads.

2¼ cups unbleached flour
2 tablespoons yellow cornmeal
1 teaspoon baking powder
½ teaspoon baking soda
¼ teaspoon salt
1 large egg
½ cup plain nonfat yogurt

½ cup (1 stick) unsalted butter or margarine
1 cup toasted walnuts, coarsely chopped
1 tablespoon finely chopped fresh rosemary leaves, or 1 teaspoon crumbled dried

In a food processor or mixer, blend the flour, cornmeal, baking powder, baking soda, and salt. Add the egg and yogurt and beat until dough is formed. Add the butter, chunks at a time, beating until just incorporated. Stir in the walnuts and rosemary.

Remove the dough from bowl and place it on a floured board. Knead it several times, and let it stand covered with a kitchen towel for 5 minutes. Divide the dough in half and shape on a lightly greased baking sheet into two logs about 2 inches wide, 15 inches long, and ⅝ to ¾ inches high. Place them 3 inches apart. Bake at 325 degrees for 20 to 25 minutes or until pale golden. Cool for 10 minutes. Transfer to a cutting board and cut each log diagonally into ½-inch slices. Place the slices cut side down on a baking sheet and toast in a 275-degree oven for 10 minutes on each side or until crispy. Cool.

Yields about 3 to 3½ dozen biscotti

Low-Fat Rosemary-Currant Biscotti

Many people like the soft, cookielike biscotti that butter yields but they don't like the fat. Here the butter remains but egg whites and whole egg substitutes reduce fat.

¼ cup (½ stick) unsalted butter	¼ teaspoon almond extract
1 cup sugar	¼ cup minced fresh rosemary
3 egg whites (2 for recipe, 1 for glaze)	3 cups flour
¼ cup egg substitute	1 tablespoon baking powder
2 teaspoons vanilla extract	¼ teaspoon salt
	⅔ cup currants

Cream together the butter and sugar until light and creamy. Beat in 2 of the egg whites until blended. Beat in the egg substitute, vanilla and almond extracts, and 2 tablespoons minced rosemary until well blended. Add the flour, baking powder, and salt and blend until smooth. Blend in the currants.

Divide the dough in half and shape on a lightly greased baking sheet into two logs about 3 inches wide and ⅝ to ¾ inches high. Roll each log in 1 teaspoon minced rosemary. Place them 3 inches apart. Lightly beat the remaining egg white and brush on the tops and sides of the logs. Bake in a 350-degree oven for 25 to 30 minutes or until they are golden brown. Cool for 10 minutes. Transfer to a cutting board and cut each log diagonally into ¾-inch slices. Place the slices cut side down on a baking sheet and toast each side in a 275-degree oven for 10 minutes. Cool.

Yields about 2 dozen biscotti

Tarragon-Thyme-Walnut Biscotti

This combination of flavors puts a new light on biscotti. Serve them with meat dishes (soft enough to eat as a hearty bread) and for dipping into hot soups on a winter evening.

½ cup (1 stick) unsalted
    butter or margarine
1 teaspoon dried tarragon
    or 1 tablespoon chopped
    fresh
1 teaspoon dried thyme or
    1 tablespoon chopped
    fresh

2 large eggs
¼ cup nonfat milk
2 cups unbleached flour
¼ cup whole wheat flour
2 teaspoons baking powder
⅛ teaspoon salt
1 cup toasted walnuts,
    coarsely chopped

Beat together the butter, tarragon, thyme, and eggs. Stir in the milk. Add the flours, baking powder, and salt and beat until the mixture thickens. Stir in the walnuts.

Shape the dough on a lightly greased baking sheet into one log about 15 inches long, 6 inches wide, and ½ inch high so you can cut these into long breadstick lengths. Bake in a 350-degree oven for 25 minutes or until they are lightly browned. Remove from oven and cool for 10 minutes. Transfer to a cutting board and cut into ¾-inch strips. Cut diagonally for longer strips, straight across for shorter pieces. Lay the slices cut side down on a baking sheet and toast in a 275-degree oven for 10 minutes on each side or until lightly browned, dry, and firm to the touch. Cool.

Yields 1½ dozen 8-inch biscotti

Red Wine Biscotti

Biscotti *di vino rosso,* or red wine, are marvelous with meats and salads or served with a cheese and fruit platter at the end of the meal. They're not as sweet as dessert biscotti.

2½ cups all-purpose flour
½ cup sugar
1½ teaspoons baking powder
⅛ teaspoon salt
1 teaspoon freshly ground black pepper
1¼ cups red wine (Cabernet, Merlot, Burgundy)

¾ cup olive oil

1 egg white, beaten until foamy
1 tablespoon lightly toasted sesame seeds

Combine the flour, sugar, baking powder, salt, and pepper in a large bowl or food processor bowl. Add the wine and olive oil and mix until smooth.

Remove the dough from the bowl and place it on a lightly greased baking sheet. Divide the dough in half and shape into two rectangular logs about 10 inches long, 3 inches wide, and ¾ inches high. Place them 3 inches apart. Brush with the beaten egg white and sprinkle with the sesame seeds. Bake at 350 degrees for 30 minutes or until lightly browned. Cool for 10 minutes. Transfer to a cutting board and cut each log into ½-inch slices. Turn off the oven, stand the slices top side up on a baking sheet, and return to the oven for a light crisping as the oven cools down. Cool before storing.

Yields 1½ dozen biscotti

Basil Pine Nut–Olive Biscotti

Serve these dainty dipping crackerlike biscotti with spicy dips or hot or cold soups.

3 tablespoons unsalted butter or margarine	1 cup toasted pine nuts
½ cup grated Parmesan cheese	2 cups all-purpose flour
2 teaspoons crumbled dried basil leaves	2 teaspoons baking powder
1 teaspoon lemon zest	1 cup pitted, drained, and blotted black olives, sliced
2 large eggs	1 beaten egg white
½ cup nonfat milk	2 tablespoons lightly toasted sesame seeds

In a large bowl or food processor bowl, beat together the butter, cheese, basil, lemon zest, and eggs. Stir in the milk, then the nuts. Add the flour and baking powder and blend.

Remove the dough from the bowl and place it on a lightly greased baking sheet. Divide the dough in half and shape into two long thin rectangles about 3 inches wide and ¼ inch high. Lay the olives onto the dough and roll it into logs 2½ to 3 inches wide and ¾ inches thick. Place them 3 inches apart. Brush the tops with the beaten egg white and sprinkle with the sesame seeds. Bake at 325 degrees for 25 to 30 minutes or until lightly browned. Cool for 10 minutes. Transfer to a cutting board and cut each log into ½-inch slices. Place the slices on a baking sheet cut side down and bake in a 275-degree oven until lightly browned, 10 minutes for each side. Cool.

Yields about 2 dozen biscotti

Biscotti de Provence

The French make a double-baked sweet cookie called *croquet de car-cassonne;* so here's a recipe based on the regional cooking of southern France, adding herbes de Provence (available in jars in supermarkets or gourmet food shops). Brush with egg white or spray with nonstick vegetable spray for a glazed top.

½ cup (1 stick) unsalted
   butter or margarine
2 large eggs
¼ cup nonfat milk
2 tablespoons dried herbes
   de Provence

2½ cups unbleached flour
2 teaspoons baking powder
⅛ teaspoon salt
½ cup sunflower seeds

Beat together the butter and eggs. Stir in the milk and add the herbes de Provence. Add the flour, baking powder, and salt and beat until the mixture thickens. Stir in the sunflower seeds.

Divide the dough in half and shape on a lightly greased baking sheet into two logs about 2½ to 3 inches wide and ¾ inches high. Place them 3 inches apart. Bake in a 350-degree oven for 20 minutes or until they are lightly browned. Cool for 10 minutes. Transfer to a cutting board and cut diagonally into ½- to ¾-inch slices. Lay the slices cut side down on the baking sheet and toast each side in a 275-degree oven for 10 minutes or until golden brown, dry, and firm to the touch.

Yields about 2 dozen biscotti

Hazelnut-Anise Biscotti

These crunchy dry cookies are excellent for scooping up vegetable dips as well as dunking into wines and coffees.

3/4 cup sugar
1/4 cup (1/2 stick) unsalted
   butter or margarine
3 large eggs
1 teaspoon vanilla extract
3 cups all-purpose flour
1 teaspoon baking powder
1/2 teaspoon baking soda
1/8 teaspoon salt

1 cup toasted chopped
   hazelnuts
1/4 cup crushed aniseed
   (with mortar and pestle,
   or place in a small
   plastic bag and smash
   with the bottom edge of a
   heavy pan)

Cream together the sugar and butter until fluffy. Mix in the eggs and vanilla. Add the flour, baking powder, baking soda, and salt and blend until smooth. Fold in the hazelnuts and aniseed.

Divide the dough in half and shape on a lightly greased baking sheet into two logs about 4 inches wide and 5/8 to 3/4 inches high. Place them 3 inches apart. Bake at 350 degrees for 25 to 30 minutes or until golden brown. Cool for 10 minutes. Transfer to a cutting board and cut each log into 3/4-inch slices. Place the slices cut side down on a baking sheet and toast each side in a 275-degree oven for 10 minutes. Cool.

Yields about 2 dozen biscotti

Pesto Biscotti

A favorite with Italian meals, soups, and salads. Top with goat cheese or mozzarella for a savory appetizer. Garnish with crushed fresh or dried basil leaves.

1 cup homemade or pur-
  chased pesto
6 tablespoons (¾ stick)
  unsalted butter or
  margarine

2 large eggs
¼ cup milk
2 cups all-purpose flour
2 teaspoons baking powder
⅛ teaspoon salt

In a large bowl or food processor bowl, beat together the pesto, butter, eggs, and milk. Add the flour, baking powder, and salt and mix until dough forms.

Remove the dough from the bowl and place it on a lightly greased baking sheet. Divide the dough in half and shape into two logs about 3 inches wide and ⅝ to ¾ inches high. Place them 3 inches apart. Bake at 350 degrees for 25 to 30 minutes or until golden brown. Cool for 10 minutes. Transfer to a cutting board and cut each log diagonally into ¾-inch slices. Place the slices cut side down on a baking sheet and toast each side in a 275-degree oven for 10 minutes. Cool.

Yields about 2½ dozen biscotti

CHAPTER

6

Biscotti

from

Around the

World

Chocolate Chip–Almond Mandelbrot

Mandelbrot, a Yiddish word meaning "almond bread," is a favorite during many Jewish holidays. Every European Jewish community boasted a slightly different, and favorite, version in times past and today's many Jewish cookbooks reflect the recipe variations. This one is easily mixed in one bowl with a wooden spoon. Mandelbrot are usually shorter than biscotti, so make the logs about 1½ to 2 inches wide.

1½ cups sugar	½ teaspoon baking soda
4 large eggs	⅛ teaspoon salt
1 cup vegetable oil	1½ cups mini semisweet
1 teaspoon vanilla extract	chocolate chips
4 cups all-purpose flour	1 cup toasted sliced
½ teaspoon baking powder	almonds

Beat together the sugar, eggs, oil, and vanilla until well blended. Add 3 cups of the flour with the baking powder, baking soda, and salt and blend. Add the chocolate chips and almonds. Add up to 1 cup more flour to make a moderately thick batter.

Divide the dough into fourths and shape on a lightly greased and floured baking sheet into four logs, each about 12 inches long, 1½ to 2 inches wide, and ⅝ to ¾ inches high. Place them 2 inches apart. Bake in a 350-degree oven for 25 minutes or until they are lightly browned. Cool for 10 minutes. Transfer to a cutting board and cut each log diagonally into ½- to ¾-inch slices. Place the slices cut side down on the baking sheet and toast each side in a 200-degree oven for 10 minutes or until golden brown. Cool.

Yields 5 to 6 dozen mandelbrot

Harriet's Jelly-Filled Mandelbrot

Here's my sister-in-law's favorite mandelbrot recipe. It's colorful and so easy to make using your favorite preserves.

1/2 cup (1 stick) unsalted butter or margarine	1 teaspoon baking powder
1 cup granulated sugar	1/8 teaspoon salt
3 large eggs	1 teaspoon ground cinnamon
1 teaspoon vanilla extract	3/4 cup strawberry preserves
2 teaspoons amaretto liqueur	3/4 cup apricot preserves
3 cups unbleached or all-purpose flour	1/4 cup confectioners' sugar

Cream together the butter and sugar until fluffy. Add the eggs one at a time, then add the vanilla and amaretto until well blended. Add the flour, baking powder, salt, and cinnamon and blend until smooth.

Divide the dough into fourths and shape on a lightly greased baking sheet into four logs about 2½ inches wide and ¾ inches high. Place them 2 inches apart. Make a trough down the center of each log. Fill two logs with strawberry preserves, the other two with apricot preserves (or another favorite flavor). Bake at 325 degrees for 20 to 25 minutes. Cool for 10 minutes. Transfer to a cutting board and cut each log diagonally into ¾-inch slices. Stand the slices up on the baking sheet and toast at 200 degrees for 10 minutes or until the tops are lightly browned. Cool. Sprinkle with confectioners' sugar.

Yields 5 to 6 dozen mandelbrot

Mandelbrot with Cake Meal

These are made with cake meal and potato starch.

1½ cups sugar
½ pound (2 sticks)
  margarine
6 large eggs
2¾ cups matzo cake meal
½ teaspoon salt
¾ cup potato starch
¾ cup chocolate chips

1 cup toasted walnuts,
  coarsely chopped

TOPPING
1 teaspoon ground
  cinnamon
2 tablespoons sugar

Cream together the 1½ cups sugar and the margarine. Add the eggs and beat well. Combine the cake meal, salt, and potato starch and fold into the creamed mixture, stirring until smooth. Add the chocolate and nuts.

Divide the dough into thirds or fourths and shape on a lightly greased baking sheet into logs about 2 inches wide and ⅝ to ¾ inches high. Place them 2 inches apart. Sprinkle with the cinnamon mixed with 2 tablespoons sugar. Bake in a 350-degree oven for 25 minutes or until they are lightly browned. Cool for 10 minutes. Transfer to a cutting board and cut each log diagonally into ½- to ¾-inch slices. Place the slices cut side down on a baking sheet and toast each side for 10 minutes in a 200-degree oven. Cool.

Yields 5 to 6 dozen mandelbrot

Mandelbrot from Poland

Here's an Old World Polish recipe updated.

¼ cup (½ stick) unsalted
butter or margarine
¼ cup brandy or whiskey
1 cup sugar
2 large eggs
2 teaspoons finely diced
orange rind
2 teaspoons orange extract
1 teaspoon vanilla extract
3 cups unbleached or
all-purpose flour

1½ teaspoons baking powder
⅛ teaspoon salt
1 cup butterscotch morsels
1 cup pistachio nuts,
coarsely chopped

TOPPING
1 teaspoon ground
cinnamon
2 tablespoons sugar

Beat together the butter, brandy, and sugar until fluffy. Add the eggs, orange rind, and orange and vanilla extracts. Blend in the flour, baking powder, and salt. Fold in butterscotch and nuts. Chill the dough for about 10 minutes or until it is no longer sticky.

Divide the dough into fourths and shape on a lightly greased baking sheet into four logs about 2 inches wide and ⅝ to ¾ inches high. Place them 3 inches apart. Bake in a 350-degree oven for 25 minutes or until they are lightly browned. For the topping, mix the cinnamon and sugar and sprinkle on the tops after baking for 15 minutes, then continue baking. Cool for 10 minutes. On a cutting board, cut each log diagonally into ½- to ¾-inch slices. Turn the oven off, return the slices to the oven, and let them dry as the oven cools.

Yields 5 to 6 dozen mandelbrot

Duotone Holiday Mandelbrot

These festive-looking mandelbrot combining chocolate and vanilla are a delicious, dainty dessert for winding up a heavy holiday meal.

2 large eggs
1 cup sugar
¾ cup vegetable oil
1 teaspoon almond
    flavoring or lemon juice
3 cups matzo cake meal
1 teaspoon baking soda

⅛ teaspoon salt
1 cup toasted sliced
    almonds
1 tablespoon unsweetened
    cocoa
2 tablespoons confectioners'
    sugar

Beat the eggs with the sugar until light and fluffy. Mix in the oil and flavoring. Add the cake meal, baking soda, and salt until well blended. Stir in the almonds. Remove two-thirds of the batter onto a lightly greased baking sheet. Add the cocoa to the remaining third in the bowl.

Shape the white dough into a long log about 3 inches wide and ½ inch high. (Cut it in half if too long for the baking sheet and place them 2 inches apart.) Roll the chocolate dough into a coil the length of each white log and about 2 inches wide and lay it along the center of the white log. Lift the edges of the white dough over the chocolate to enclose it. Bake in a 350-degree oven for 25 minutes or until lightly browned. Cool for 10 minutes. Transfer to a cutting board and cut diagonally into ½- to ¾-inch slices. Lay the slices on a baking sheet and toast each side in a 200-degree oven for 10 minutes. Cool. Sprinkle with confectioners' sugar.

Yields 3 to 4 dozen mandelbrot

Sesame-Almond Passover Mandelbrot

Sesame seeds and almonds give this mandelbrot a nice crunch!

¾ cup vegetable oil
¾ cup sugar
3 large eggs
¾ cup matzo cake meal
¼ cup matzo meal
2 tablespoons potato starch
½ teaspoon salt
1½ teaspoons ground
  cinnamon
1 tablespoon lemon juice

2 tablespoons lemon zest
1 cup toasted sliced almonds
⅓ cup sesame seeds

TOPPING
2 tablespoons sugar
½ teaspoon ground
  cinnamon

2 tablespoons confectioners'
  sugar

Blend the oil and sugar in a large mixing bowl. Add the eggs and blend thoroughly. Combine the cake meal, matzo meal, starch, salt, and cinnamon and blend into oil mixture with the lemon juice and zest. Fold in the almonds and sesame seeds. Refrigerate for 30 minutes.

Divide the dough into two or three parts and shape into logs 2 inches wide and 1 inch high. Place them 2 inches apart on greased baking sheets. Bake at 350 degrees for 25 minutes or until golden brown. Cool for 10 minutes. Transfer to a cutting board and cut each log into ½- to ¾-inch slices. For the topping, mix and sprinkle with the sugar-cinnamon mixture. Lay the slices on a baking sheet cut side up and toast on each side in a 200-degree oven for 10 minutes or until golden brown. Cool. Sprinkle with confectioners' sugar.

Yields 4 dozen mandelbrot

Spanish Mandelbrot

Sephardic Jews transported mandelbrot from their home countries to Spain and created this cookie with anise, almonds, and sesame seeds.

¼ cup vegetable oil (or unsalted butter or margarine)

1 cup sugar

3 large eggs

2 teaspoons anise extract or anisette liqueur

3¼ cups flour

2 teaspoons baking powder

⅛ teaspoon salt

½ cup crushed aniseed (with a mortar and pestle, or place in plastic bag and crush with the bottom edge of a heavy pan)

1 cup toasted sliced almonds

1 egg white

½ cup sesame seeds

Blend the oil and sugar thoroughly. Add the eggs, and anise flavoring and beat well. Add the flour, baking powder, salt, and aniseed and blend until smooth. Fold in the almonds.

Divide the dough into thirds and shape on a lightly greased baking sheet into three logs about 2 inches wide and ⅝ to ¾ inches high. Place them 2 inches apart. Beat the egg white, brush over the logs, and sprinkle with sesame seeds. Bake in a 350-degree oven for 20 to 25 minutes or until they are lightly browned. Cool for 10 minutes. Transfer to a cutting board and cut each log diagonally into ½- to ¾-inch slices. Place the slices cut side down on a baking sheet and toast each side in a 250-degree oven for 10 minutes or until lightly browned. Cool.

Yields 3 to 3½ dozen mandelbrot

Greek Paximadia

Greek biscotti, called *paximadia,* have several variations usually flavored with aniseed—from an herb of the carrot family that has a licorice taste and aroma. You can substitute walnuts or hazelnuts for the almonds for variety.

3/4 cup sugar
1/4 cup (1/2 stick) unsalted
  butter
3 large eggs
1 tablespoon crushed
  aniseed or 2 teaspoons
  anise extract
3 tablespoons grated orange
  peel

3 tablespoons grated lemon
  peel
3 cups all-purpose flour
1 1/2 teaspoons baking powder
1/2 teaspoon baking soda
1/2 teaspoon salt
1 1/2 cups toasted sliced
  almonds

Cream together the sugar and butter. Add the eggs. Mix in the aniseed and orange and lemon peels. Add the flour, baking powder, baking soda, and salt and blend well. Fold in the almonds.

Divide the dough in half and shape on a lightly greased baking sheet into two logs about 3½ inches wide and ⅝ to ¾ inches high. Place them 2 inches apart. Bake in a 350-degree oven for 15 to 20 minutes or until they are lightly browned. Cool for 10 minutes. Transfer to a cutting board and cut each log diagonally into ½- to ¾-inch slices. Lay the slices cut side down on a baking sheet and toast on each side for 10 minutes in a 275-degree oven until crisp. Cool.

Yields about 3 dozen biscotti

Mixed-Heritage Biscotti

The baker who gave me this recipe claims it's a cross between Greek and Italian because olive oil and chopped walnuts are used.

2 large eggs
1 cup sugar
$\frac{1}{2}$ cup olive oil
1 teaspoon almond extract
2 teaspoons lemon zest
3 cups unbleached or
   all-purpose flour
1 teaspoon baking powder
$\frac{1}{8}$ teaspoon salt

1 teaspoon ground
   cinnamon
$\frac{1}{2}$ teaspoon nutmeg
$\frac{3}{4}$ cup chopped walnuts
$\frac{3}{4}$ cup chopped mixed dried
   fruits
$\frac{1}{4}$ cup diced candied orange
   peel

Beat the eggs, sugar, olive oil, almond extract, and lemon zest until well blended. Add the flour, baking powder, salt, cinnamon, and nutmeg and blend until smooth. Stir in the walnuts, dried fruit, and orange peel.

Divide the dough into thirds and shape on a lightly greased baking sheet into three logs about 2 inches wide and $\frac{5}{8}$ to $\frac{3}{4}$ inches high. Place them 2 inches apart. Bake in a 350-degree oven for 20 to 25 minutes or until they are lightly browned. Cool for 10 minutes. Transfer to a cutting board and cut each log diagonally into $\frac{1}{2}$- to $\frac{3}{4}$-inch slices. Stand the slices up on a baking sheet, turn off the heat, and return to the oven for about 15 minutes until toasted. Cool.

Yields 3 dozen biscotti

English Scocotti with Toffee and Currants

In England, where scones are the dry pastry of choice, restaurants and cafés are selling Italian biscotti for a teatime accompaniment. We vote for developing an English version that we're calling "scocotti," chock-full of English toffee bits (at a supermarket baking supply shelf) or chopped peanut brittle or pralines. And lots of currants, of course.

¼ cup (½ stick) unsalted butter or margarine
⅔ cup sugar
3 large eggs
1 teaspoon almond extract
3 cups unbleached or all-purpose flour

1½ teaspoons baking powder
⅛ teaspoon salt
¾ cup English toffee bits (or chopped peanut brittle or pralines)
1 cup currants

Blend the butter and sugar until fluffy. Mix in the eggs and almond extract. Add the flour, baking powder, and salt and blend well. Fold in the toffee and currants.

Divide the dough in half and shape on a lightly greased baking sheet into two logs about 3 inches wide and ⅝ to ¾ inches high. Place them 2 inches apart. Bake in a 350-degree oven for 20 minutes or until they are lightly browned. Cool for 10 minutes. Transfer to a cutting board and cut each log diagonally into ½- to ¾-inch slices. Stand the slices up on a baking sheet, turn off the heat, and return to the oven for about 20 minutes or until both sides are crisp. Cool.

Yields 3 dozen scocotti

Biscotti Piecrust,
an International Treat

Commercial biscotti bakers, reluctant to allow any waste, have discovered a way to use the broken and short biscotti pieces. Biscotti piecrust mix is available in gourmet food shops. Make your own by gathering broken small pieces, ends, and any crumbs that result along the way and keeping them in a container in the freezer. When you have enough, grind them finely in your blender or food processor to the consistency of graham cracker crumbs. Use the biscotti crumbs to make pie or tart crusts.

⅓ cup melted butter or margarine

2 cups finely ground biscotti crumbs

Mix the melted butter into the crumbs until all the crumbs are moistened. Press into the bottom and along the sides of an 8- or 9-inch pie plate. Fill with your favorite pie filling. Sprinkle crumbs on top of the pie, too.

Makes one 8- or 9-inch piecrust

Note: Also use biscotti crumbs to sprinkle on ice cream and puddings, or use them as the base for any bar cookie or recipe that calls for graham cracker crumbs.

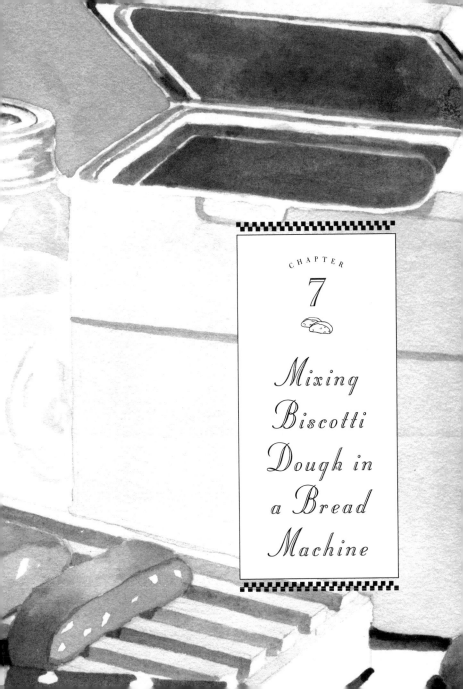

CHAPTER

7

Mixing
Biscotti
Dough in
a Bread
Machine

Mixing biscotti dough in a bread machine is easy and fast, and cleaning up is oh, so quick. It doesn't matter what size machine you have, a 1-pound, 1½- or 2-pound. You only mix the ingredients in the pan during the first part of the dough or manual cycle. Combine the dry ingredients in a large measuring cup so they are ready to pour into the pan as mixing continues. Keep the top open and add ingredients while the paddle is going, being careful to not spill any into the baking chamber.

1. Place eggs, sugar, and vanilla in the pan and set the pan in the machine. Select the dough or manual cycle, depending on your unit. Start and mix for 5 minutes (after a preheat cycle on some machines). Check the mixing cycle timing in your instruction book.

2. Add the flour and other dry ingredients to the pan and let the machine mix another 4 minutes or until dough forms.

3. Add nuts, raisins, or dried fruits and continue to mix until all are incorporated into the dough, about 3 minutes. Use a rubber spatula to push the dry ingredients into the mix if they adhere to the pan's sides.

Total mixing time in most machines is 10 to 12 minutes in the dough cycle. Turn off or unplug the machine, remove the pan from the machine, and remove the dough from the pan. If the dough is sticky, coat your hands lightly with vegetable oil or nonstick vegetable spray. Follow biscotti recipe directions for shaping, baking, and toasting.

The recipes that follow can also be made in a food processor or by hand.

Almond-Hazelnut-Chocolate Biscotti

Almost any type of unsalted nuts you have available can be combined; try walnuts, pecans, or peanuts, with almonds.

4 egg whites or 3 whole eggs	1/8 teaspoon salt
3/4 cup sugar	1/4 cup unsweetened cocoa
1/4 cup almond paste, at	powder
room temperature (see	3/4 cup coarsely chopped
page 17)	hazelnuts (or sliced
1 teaspoon vanilla extract	amonds)
3 cups unbleached flour	1 cup white chocolate
1 1/2 teaspoons baking powder	morsels

On the bread machine dough cycle, mix the eggs, sugar, and almond paste for 5 minutes; add the vanilla during the last minute. Combine and add the flour, baking powder, salt, and cocoa and continue mixing for 4 minutes. Add the nuts and chocolate morsels and mix 1 to 2 minutes longer, until they are incorporated or until the end of the mixing cycle. Stop or unplug the machine and remove the pan. Transfer the dough from the pan onto a lightly greased baking sheet.

Divide the dough in half or thirds and shape into logs about 2½ inches wide and ⅝ to ¾ inches high. Place them 3 inches apart. Bake in a 350-degree oven for 20 minutes. Cool for 10 minutes. Transfer to a cutting board and cut each log diagonally into ½- to ¾-inch slices. Place the slices cut side down on a baking sheet and toast in a 275-degree oven, 10 minutes on each side. Cool.

Yields 2½ to 3 dozen biscotti

Orange-Cranberry-Nut Biscotti

A finely textured, colorful orange and red biscotto that doubles as a cookie and looks beautiful on a buffet table.

3 large eggs
1 cup sugar
1 tablespoon vegetable oil
1 teaspoon orange extract
1 teaspoon orange zest
3 cups unbleached or
   all-purpose flour
1 teaspoon baking powder
$^{1}/_{2}$ teaspoon baking soda

$^{1}/_{8}$ teaspoon salt
$^{3}/_{4}$ cup coarsely chopped
   candied orange peels
$^{3}/_{4}$ cup dried cranberries or
   $1^{1}/_{2}$ cups fresh, coarsely
   chopped
$^{1}/_{2}$ cup toasted walnuts,
   coarsely chopped

In a bread machine pan, mix the eggs and sugar together on the dough or manual cycle for 5 minutes, adding the oil during last minute. Add the orange extract and zest. Combine and add the flour, baking powder, baking soda, and salt and continue mixing for about 4 minutes. Add the orange peels and cranberries until partially incorporated into the dough, then add the walnuts. Push the ingredients down from the pan sides into the paddle area until everything is incorporated (about 2 minutes) or until the cycle stops. If necessary, restart the machine and mix a few minutes more. Stop or unplug the machine and remove the pan. Transfer the dough from the pan onto a lightly greased baking sheet.

Divide the dough in half or thirds and shape each piece into a log about $3^{1}/_{2}$ inches wide and $^{5}/_{8}$ to $^{3}/_{4}$ inches high. Place them 3 inches apart. Bake in a 350-degree oven for 25 minutes. Cool for 10 minutes. Transfer to a cutting board and cut each log diagonally into ¾-inch slices. Place the slices cut side down on a baking sheet and toast each side in a 275-degree oven for 10 minutes or until golden brown. Cool.

Yields about 3 dozen biscotti

Southern Peanut Biscotti

Cornmeal combined with the flour gives these biscotti a crunchy texture and wonderful flavor. When combined with peanuts, the result is scrumptious. They're excellent for dipping in appetizers as well as in wine.

3 large eggs
1 cup sugar
1 teaspoon vanilla extract
2½ cups unbleached flour
1 cup yellow cornmeal

1 teaspoon baking powder
⅛ teaspoon salt
1½ cups raw, unsalted
  peanuts

In a bread machine pan, mix the eggs and sugar together on the dough or manual cycle for 5 minutes, adding the vanilla during the last minute. Combine and add the flour, cornmeal, baking powder, and salt and mix about 4 minutes, until dough forms. Add the peanuts and let the machine continue to mix for 1 to 2 minutes, until the nuts are incorporated or until the end of the mixing cycle. Stop or unplug the machine and remove the pan. Transfer the dough from the pan onto a lightly greased baking sheet.

Divide the dough in half and shape into two logs about 3 inches wide and ¾ inches high. Place them 3 inches apart. Bake in a 350-degree oven for 30 minutes. Cool for 10 minutes. Transfer to a cutting board and cut each log diagonally into ¾-inch slices. Place the slices cut side down on a baking sheet and toast each side in a 250-degree oven for 10 minutes or until lightly crisp. Cool.

Yields 2½ dozen biscotti

Heartland Granola-Raisin Biscotti

These nutritious biscotti are ideal in place of breakfast breads. Pack them in lunch boxes and backpacks for snacks any time of the day.

3 large eggs
1 cup dark brown sugar
1 teaspoon lemon extract or
*   juice*
1 teaspoon lemon zest
2 cups unbleached flour
1¼ cups granola (any flavor)

1½ teaspoons baking powder
⅛ teaspoon salt
½ cup golden raisins
½ cup dark raisins
½ cup toasted walnuts,
*   coarsely chopped*

In a bread machine pan, mix the eggs and brown sugar together on the dough or manual cycle for 5 minutes. Add the lemon extract and zest while the machine is still running. Combine and add the flour, granola, baking powder, and salt as the machine continues mixing, about 4 minutes. Add the raisins and nuts and mix until dough forms. Stop or unplug the machine and remove the pan. Transfer the dough from the pan onto a lightly greased baking sheet.

Divide the dough in half or thirds and shape each piece into a log 3 inches wide and ⅝ to ¾ inches high. Place them 3 inches apart. Bake in a 350-degree oven for 25 minutes. Cool for 10 minutes. Transfer to a cutting board. Cut each log diagonally into ½- to ¾-inch slices. Place the slices cut side down on a baking sheet and toast each side in a 275-degree oven for 10 minutes or until golden brown. Cool.

Yields 3 dozen biscotti

Date-Pistachio Biscotti

Need ideas for what to combine in biscotti? Take your cue from the ingredients given in bread machine recipe books.

3 large eggs
1 cup brown sugar
¼ cup honey
3 cups unbleached flour
1 teaspoon baking powder
½ teaspoon baking soda
⅛ teaspoon salt
½ teaspoon ground cinnamon

1 teaspoon unsweetened cocoa powder
¾ cup chopped dried dates lightly rolled in 1 tablespoon flour
½ cup lightly toasted raw pistachio nuts

In a bread machine pan, mix the eggs and brown sugar together on the dough or manual cycle for 5 minutes. Add the honey during the last minute of mixing. Combine and add the flour, baking powder, baking soda, salt, cinnamon, and cocoa and continue mixing for 4 minutes. Add the dates and pistachio nuts and mix until dough forms. Stop or unplug the machine and remove the pan. Transfer the dough from the pan onto a lightly greased baking sheet.

Divide the dough in half or thirds and shape into a log 4 inches wide and ⅝ to ¾ inches high. Place them 3 inches apart. Bake in a 350-degree oven for 25 minutes. Cool for 10 minutes. Transfer to a cutting board and cut each log diagonally into ¾-inch slices. Place the slices cut side down on a baking sheet and toast each side in a 250-degree oven for 10 minutes or until golden brown. Cool.

Yields about 3 dozen biscotti

CHAPTER

8

Dipping
Delights

Appetizers
and Stupendous Soups

Tasty, toasted gourmet herb biscotti are a wonderful partner, or replacement, for traditional bread rounds and crackers served with appetizers, soups, and cheeses.

Guacamole Biscotti Wheel

Serve guacamole, a Mexican delicacy, with any herbed biscotti.

1 large ripe avocado
1 teaspoon lemon juice
1 teaspoon Parisian spicy
   brown mustard (or other
   flavor)

½ teaspoon Tabasco sauce,
   or to taste
1 small tomato, chopped
1 basket of herbed biscotti

Scoop the avocado pulp from the shell and remove the pit. Crush the pulp in a medium-size bowl. Add the lemon juice, brown mustard, Tabasco sauce, and tomato and blend until smooth with a fork or in a blender. Lay the biscotti, wheel-like fashion, around a plate with the guacamole mounded in the center. Each person lifts a biscotti with the guacamole on one end. Or serve as a dip with any of the herbed biscotti in chapter 5.

Serves 4

Hearty Artichoke Appetizer

An easy-to-make hot appetizer that can be served in a flat dish or in a fondue pot for easy dipping.

1 jar (14 ounces) mari-
nated artichoke hearts,
drained and chopped
½ cup mayonnaise

½ cup grated Parmesan
cheese
½ teaspoon dried dill
¼ teaspoon minced garlic

Combine the ingredients in a low-rimmed casserole or a pie plate and bake at 400 degrees for about 10 minutes, or until bubbly.

Serves 8 to 10

Lemon-Avocado Soup

3 avocados
½ cup lemon juice
3 cups chicken broth

1½ cups sour cream or plain
yogurt
½ teaspoon seasoned salt
4 cherry tomatoes, sliced

Puree the avocado flesh and combine with the lemon juice and broth. Add 1 cup of the sour cream and the salt. Serve cold and garnish with the remaining sour cream and cherry tomatoes sliced into rounds.

Serves 4

Carrot-Leek Bisque

This delicious low-calorie soup can be served hot or cold and is delicious with basil-flavored biscotti cut long and thin. Stand the biscotti upright in jars or glasses for a decorative touch.

6 cups water
6 cups carrot slices
1 garlic clove, chopped
1 small onion, chopped
2 stalks celery, sliced
2 large leeks, sliced in
    rounds
1/2 teaspoon sage
1/4 teaspoon tarragon
1/4 teaspoon thyme
1 teaspoon (1 package)
    miso or 1 vegetable
    bouillon cube
2 tablespoons sour cream
    sprinkled with chopped
    chives, for garnish

Bring 6 cups of water to a boil in large (6 quart) soup pot. Add the vegetables and seasonings. Cover, bring to a boil, then turn down the heat and simmer for about 30 minutes or until the vegetables are soft. Remove 1 cup sliced carrots with a slotted spoon and set aside. Puree the remaining soup in a blender or food processor until smooth. Return the sliced carrots to the puree. Reheat and serve, or serve cold with the sour cream sprinkled with chives. The bisque can be frozen and reheated in a microwave oven or on the stovetop.

Serves 8

Colossal Coffees

Biscotti are at home with many different kinds of drinks. You can be perfectly happy dunking them in your everyday morning coffee. Or opt for more exotic flavors like those available in coffee cafés. It involves making espresso in a special espresso machine or brewing espresso beans in your coffee maker and adding steamed milk (see page 89).

When making biscotti and coffee for desserts, remember that the subtle tastes of different biscotti can be overpowered by strong coffees. With that as a warning, here are coffee flavors our testers recommend.

ESPRESSO

"Espresso" coffee describes both the blend of beans and the process used to prepare it. The espresso roast bean blend results in one of the darkest coffee roasts and has a slightly burnt flavor. It should be ground to about the texture of fine breadcrumbs. For the process, a special espresso machine that uses pressure extracts the essence of the coffee from the finely ground bean. However, some espresso coffee is sold to be brewed in home coffee makers.

After the espresso is brewed, steamed milk can slowly be poured into the coffee and topped with the foam produced by the steamed milk giving you a cappuccino.

Espresso tastes best served in thin china or glass cups; never serve it in plastic or paper cups.

Some popular espresso based coffee drinks follow. Combine the ingredients in the order given. Top with cinnamon, nutmeg, chocolate powder, or whipped cream.

Cappuccino

$^1/_3$ *cup espresso* $^1/_3$ *cup foamed milk*
$^1/_2$ *cup hot steamed milk*

Top with cinnamon, nutmeg, or chocolate powder.

Serves 1

Caffè Latte

1 cup steamed milk   *A shot of espresso to taste*

Top with a thin layer of foamed milk sprinkled with cinnamon, nutmeg, or chocolate powder.

Serves 1

Café Mocha

$^1/_3$ *cup espresso*   *2 tablespoons chocolate*
$^2/_3$ *cup steamed milk*   *syrup*

Top with whipped cream sprinkled with chocolate powder.

Serves 1

Making Steamed Milk

Machines for making steamed milk are used in coffee shops and restaurants. Using steam pressure, they introduce air into milk to double or triple the milk's volume and produce froth.

Steamed milk can be made at home on the stovetop. Nonfat milk froths more easily than low-fat and whole milk, but low-fat milk produces a smoother, creamier foam. Use small amounts of milk: about ½ cup for two servings. Heat the milk only until steaming (about 150 degrees; test it with an instant-read thermometer), being careful not to scorch it.

There are several inexpensive devices for making steamed milk that cost less than $50. Espresso makers for the home that both brew the coffee and make the steamed milk and froth range in prices from about $50 to $500.

Pour ½ cup cold milk (for 2 cups of espresso) into a small saucepan over medium-high heat on a stovetop burner, and whisk with a large wire whisk. The milk will become frothy and about double in size, and steam will appear. It takes about 5 minutes and the milk will reach a temperature of 140 to 150 degrees. Use as soon as possible, but it can be kept warm over medium heat. Keep whisking to retain the froth.

Once you have the froth, pour the hot milk layer from beneath into the coffee and spoon the foam on the coffee surface.

Dessert Debaucheries

Biscotti can give a dish of plain ice cream, gelato, or yogurt an international flair. Garnish ice-cream dishes with sweet biscotti instead of the usual wafers or cookies. Biscotti also taste great dipped into your favorite fondue.

Mocha Soda

This is delicious served on a hot summer day with almond chocolate biscotti.

4 egg whites
$\frac{1}{2}$ cup sugar
1 teaspoon instant espresso powder
2 cups strong brewed coffee, cold

Dutch chocolate ice cream
4 tablespoons rum or brandy (optional)

Beat the egg whites until soft peaks form. Gradually beat in the sugar and espresso powder to a meringue consistency. Pour $\frac{1}{2}$ cup of the cold coffee into each of four tall glasses. Spoon in a layer of meringue, sealing it against the sides of glass to keep the coffee from rising. Gently top with two large scoops of ice cream. Pour a tablespoon of rum or brandy on top.

Serves 4

Chocolate Espresso Cream Parfait

4 cups miniature
   marshmallows
1 ounce unsweetened
   chocolate

1 cup (8 ounces) espresso or
   strong coffee
1 cup heavy cream
8 biscotti

Melt the marshmallows and chocolate in the coffee in a microwave or double boiler and stir until the marshmallows are melted. Chill the mixture until almost set. Whip the heavy cream until stiff peaks form, then fold two-thirds of the cream into the chilled mixture. Spoon into parfait glasses, layering wide portions of chocolate with one or two thinner layers of the remaining whipped cream. Top with a dollop of whipped cream and serve with 2 biscotti.

Serves 4

Easy Rum Floats

1 pint vanilla ice cream
½ cup rum

2 cups brewed espresso
   coffee
A dish full of biscotti

Place 2 scoops of ice cream and 2 tablespoons rum in each of 2 tall glasses. Slowly pour coffee into each glass and serve with biscotti for stirring and dipping. Straws are suggested, too.

Serves 2

Winning Dipping Wines and Liqueurs

Suggested sweet dessert wines for dipping are appropriate for winding up a book on biscotti. They range from light pink and white to ruby or tawny varieties. Liqueurs can be delicious as a dipping medium, too. Irish Cream with an almond biscotto is delectable.

Aquavit	*Orvieto*
Bordeaux	*Rubesco*
Cherry Heering	*Sauternes*
Chianti	*Tequila*
Frascati	*Tokay*
Irish Cream	*Verducchio*
Kahlúa	*Vino Rosso*
Madeira	*Vin Santo*
Muscatel	*Zinfandel*

Toasts

Finally, a few toasts—not the biscotti kind but the "To your health" kind—from different countries. Add a few of your own to those below.

L'Chaim—*Hebrew*	Santé—*France*
Prosit—*Germany*	Skoal—*Scandinavia*
Salud—*Mexico*	Egészségére—*Hungary*
Salute—*Italy*	Gan-Bay—*China*

$\mathcal{D}irectory$

Information Sources—Suppliers

Need information? Look for telephone numbers listed on packages. The following companies have speciality baking and food products including coffee machines, bread machines, food processors, mixers, and hard-to-find baking supplies. Many carry flours, grains, dried fruits, nuts, spices, coffees, teas, and everything else you need to make and enjoy exotically flavored biscotti. Several have booklets, help sheets, and catalogs for the asking.

The Chef's Catalog
3215 Commercial Ave.
Northbrook, IL 60052
800-338-3232

General Mills, Inc.
Gold Medal Flour
Box 200-SP
Minneapolis, MN 55440
800-328-6787

King Arthur Flour
Baker's Catalogue
Box 1010
Norwich, VT 05055
800-827-6836

K-TEC
420 N. Geneva Rd.
Linden, UT 84042
800-288-6455

The Great Valley Mills
R.D. 3, County Line Rd.
Box 1111
Barto, PA 19504
800-688-6455

Walnut Acres
Penns Creek, PA 17862
800-433-3998

Index

Conversion Chart

American cooks use standard containers, the 8-ounce cup and a tablespoon that takes exactly 16 level fillings to fill that cup level. Measuring by cup makes it very difficult to give weight equivalents, as a cup of densely packed butter will weigh considerably more than a cup of flour. The easiest way therefore to deal with cup measurements in recipes is to take the amount by volume rather than by weight. Thus the equation reads:

$$1 \text{ cup} = 240 \text{ ml} = 8 \text{ fl. oz.} \quad \tfrac{1}{2} \text{ cup} = 120 \text{ ml} = 4 \text{ fl. oz.}$$

It is possible to buy a set of American cup measures in major stores around the world.

In the States, butter is often measured in sticks. One stick is the equivalent of 8 tablespoons. One tablespoon of butter is therefore the equivalent to ½ ounce/15 grams.

Liquid Measures

Fluid ounces	U.S.	Imperial	Milliliters
	1 tsp	1 tsp	5
¼	2 tsp	1 dessertspoon	10
½	1 tbs	1 tbs	14
1	2 tbs	2 tbs	28
2	¼ cup	4 tbs	56
4	½ cup		110
5		¼ pint or 1 gill	140
6	¾ cup		170
8	1 cup		225
9			250, ¼ liter
10	1¼ cups	½ pint	280
12	1½ cups		340
15		¾ pint	420
16	2 cups		450
18	2¼ cups		500, ½ liter
20	2½ cups	1 pint	560
24	3 cups		675
25		1¼ pints	700
27	3½ cups		750
30	3¾ cups	1½ pints	840
32	4 cups or 1 quart		900

Solid Measures

U.S. and Imperial Measures		Metric Measures	
ounces	pounds	grams	kilos
1		28	
2		56	
3½		100	
4	¼	112	
5		140	
6		168	
8	½	225	
9		250	¼
12	¾	340	
16	1	450	
18		500	½
20	1¼	560	
24	1½	675	
27		750	¾
28	1¾	780	
32	2	900	
36	2¼	1000	1
40	2½	1100	
48	3	1350	
54		1500	1½
64	4	1800	
72	4½	2000	2
80	5	2250	2¼
90		2500	2½
100	6	2800	2¾